# Let's Say Grace

# Let's Say Grace

## Mealtime Prayers for Family Occasions Throughout the Year

### Robert M. Hamma

AVE MARIA PRESS
NOTRE DAME, INDIANA 46556

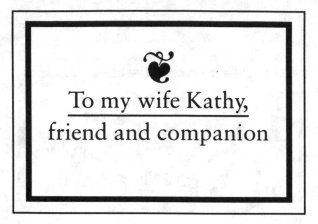

To my wife Kathy,
friend and companion

©1995 by Ave Maria Press, Inc.

International Standard Book Number: 0-87793-555-6

Library of Congress Catalog Card Number: 95-78470

Cover, text design and illustrations by Katherine Robinson Coleman

Printed and bound in the United States of America.

# CONTENTS

# INTRODUCTION

Recently, I invited my son's friend Mark to stay for dinner. When we joined hands to say grace, he looked perplexed, but went along with it. When we finished our brief prayer, he said, "We don't say a prayer before we eat at my house . . . we're Catholic."

While I laughed to myself at the time, I later recalled that Mark's upbringing was probably much like mine. While I received all the ingredients of a good Catholic education, grace before meals was a rare event at my house. When I saw the Martin family say grace on Lassie, I assumed they were Protestant.

Yet now that I have children of my own, I have come to value a brief prayer before dinner, not only for their sake, but for mine as well. It's an opportunity to stop and remember God's presence in the events of the day, to be grateful for the gift of food before us, and to remember those who are in need. When, in the course of our blessing, we acknowledge the gift of a beautiful day, bless a child on his birthday, praise a family member for her special achievement, or pray for a friend who is visiting, we are remembering that God is with us—not only at this meal—but all day long. While prayer at table is not the only time a family can or should pray, it is perhaps the most natural and easiest time. Despite our intentions to pray together as a family on other occasions, this is the one form of prayer that we have managed to make a consistent part of our family life.

Naturally, everyone does not always participate whole-heartedly or cheerfully, and the meal that follows the prayer often has a fair share of raucous behavior, teasing, spilt milk, and frayed tempers. Nevertheless, that moment of calm at the beginning sets a tone of gratitude and calls us to think briefly about the person whose hand is in ours as we pray.

A recent experience at a friend's house brought this home to me. While I sat waiting for a signal to begin the meal, our two-year-old daughter reached out and took the hand of the child next to her. When the child asked why Sarah had done that, we explained our family custom. Then we all joined hands and prayed the familiar words, "God is great, God is good, let us thank God for this food." As smiles of embarrassment broke out around the table, I marvelled at the way Sarah, who was not yet old enough to know the words of the prayer, had helped us let down our guard and open up to God's presence in each other.

Jesus' presence at meals seems to have had the same effect. All the gospels record how frequently Jesus took the opportunity of a shared meal to teach, to challenge, to comfort, and to forgive. But even more importantly, all of Jesus' meals were an opportunity for his companions to open their hearts to him, to recognize him as the two disciples from the road to Emmaus did when he broke bread with them.

This was true regardless of who his dining companions were. Outcasts like Zacchaeus the tax collector, powerful people like Simon the Pharisee, or friends and disciples like Martha and Mary all experienced meals with Jesus that brought about important changes in their lives. I imagine that, if we could ask people who actually knew Jesus about their most memorable moment with him, many would say, "It was that time when we were eating and he. . . ." Perhaps that is part of the reason Jesus left us the gesture of sharing bread and wine in the eucharist as the best way to remember him, saying, "Do this in memory of me."

We can remember him not only at the eucharistic table of the altar, but at our family tables as well. While every one of our family meals won't have the same dramatic effect as the meals Jesus shared with people like Zacchaeus or Martha, they certainly make a difference over the long run. The regular practice of saying grace helps create an atmosphere where gratitude to God, respect for one another, and concern for those in need can grow.

Hopefully, the prayers in this book will provide a way to nurture those attitudes in our homes. The eight chapters offer prayers for the days of the week, for the seasons of the church year, for religious holy days (including special remembrances of the saints) and national holidays, and for significant family occasions (like birthdays, anniversaries, or the beginning of school). There is also a chapter with traditional graces and meal blessings that can be used any time.

These mealtime prayers help us celebrate the unique moments in our family's life, whether it be a visit by grandma and grandpa or the night of a dance recital. But they also aim to help us look beyond our family circle to the larger circles to which we all belong: the circle of the church, the circle of our nation, and the circle of all creation. Remembering people like St. Francis, Dorothy Day, or Martin Luther King helps us to reach out through time to connect with the inspiring witness of those who came before us. Recalling the needs of those who are hungry, suffering, or oppressed stirs us to consider what we can do to share our wealth. Observing the first day of summer or the first snowfall reminds us that our meals are indeed the fruit of the earth.

Praying at table can lead us gradually to recognize that Jesus is indeed at the center of all these circles of family and friends, church and neighborhood, the world and all its creatures. Thus when we pray and eat, Jesus is truly present with us.

# ORDINARY

## DAYS

# Sunday

God our Creator,
we thank you for this Sunday.
We thank you for our church,
for our home, and for the chance to rest today.
As we share this meal help us to recognize
the presence of Jesus with us
and fill us with the joy of your Holy Spirit.
We ask this through Christ our Lord.
Amen.

# Monday

We thank you God
for this new week which we have begun today.
We thank you for our schools and for our work,
and for all our friends there.
Bless this food which we share
and give us the strength
to be patient and kind with one another.
Amen.

# Tuesday

Dear God,
your love is like a mother's gentle hands
and your care is like a father's watchful presence.
We thank you for always being there for us
and for giving us the gift of each other as a family.
During this meal help us listen to one another
and appreciate each one's special gifts.
We ask this in Jesus' name.
Amen.

# Wednesday

Generous God,
we give you thanks for this food
and for all the good things you have given us.
Help us to remember those who are hungry tonight.
Teach us how we can help all those who are in need.
We ask this through Christ our Lord.
Amen.

# Thursday

Blessed are you, Lord our God.
You made the land, the sea, the sun, and the rain.
You brought forth this food from nature's bounty to our table.
We thank you for the farmers who grew it
and for the many people who brought it
from the fields to the factories to the supermarkets.
And we thank you for (name) who cooked it for us.
Amen.

# Friday

Loving God,
as we come to the end of another week of work and school,
we thank you for your friendship
and ask your forgiveness for our failings.
Help us to be more like Jesus
who showed us his love on the cross.
And make us grateful for all your gifts
and for this meal we now share.
Amen.

# Saturday

Lord Jesus,
you are with us always
in our chores and in our play,
in what we do together,
and when we are apart.
Help us to grow in love as a family
and to be a sign of your presence
to our friends and neighbors.
Thank you for this food and for this day.
Amen.

# SPECIAL
## DAYS

# Mom's Birthday

Dear God,
we thank you for Mom,
especially on her birthday.
Thank you for the many ways
she takes such good care of us,
and for her patience and understanding.
Through her love we feel your presence.
Listen now to our prayers:
(each person offers a short prayer for her).
Loving God, bless Mom
and bless this meal which we share to celebrate her life.
Amen.

# Dad's Birthday

Dear God,
we thank you for giving us
such a good Dad.
As we celebrate his birthday,
we remember all the ways that he cares for us and helps us:
(each person names something about Dad that he or she is grateful for).
Loving God,
we ask you to bless Dad with your strength and wisdom,
and we thank you for this meal which we share as a family.
Amen.

# Child's Birthday

Dear Jesus,
thank you for giving us (name)
to be part of our family.
As we celebrate his/her birthday
we ask you to be with him/her as a friend
and to guide him/her as he/she grows in the year ahead.
(Here each one can thank God
for a special quality that the birthday person possesses.)
Now, dear Lord, bless this meal
which we share to celebrate (name's)  life.
Amen.

# Wedding Anniversary

(to be read by one of the children)

God of love,
thank you for this day
when we celebrate Mom and Dad's wedding anniversary.
You brought them together
and from their love our family has grown.
We thank you for their love
and ask you to give them the help they need
to love each other even more.
Help us to remember their needs too,
and not just think of our own.
Strengthen us as a family
and bless this food
as we share it together.
We ask this in Jesus' name.
Amen.

# Anniversary of a Baptism

(use the child's baptismal candle and a photo from the baptism)

God our Creator,
thank you for the gift of (name)
and for life of Jesus which lives within him/her.
Today we remember his/her baptism,
how through water and the Holy Spirit
he/she became your child
and a member of your family, the church.
Help (name) to continue to grow in your love.
Bring him/her closer to you each day
so he/she can make your light shine forth for all of us.
Bless this food which we share
in the name of Jesus, our friend and brother.
Amen.

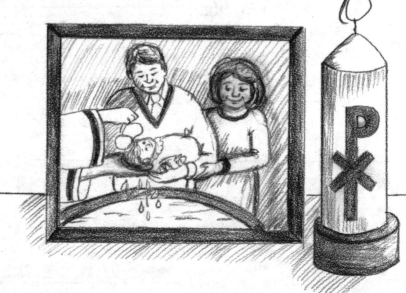

## When Friends Visit

Lord Jesus,
as we gather together for this meal
we remember your words to your first disciples,
"I call you my friends."
We remember the many meals you shared with your friends,
sometimes wonderful banquets,
sometimes simple meals eaten outdoors.
Be with us now as we share this meal with our friends in your name.
May our sharing of this food and drink deepen our friendship
and help us to appreciate your presence in one another.
We ask this with trust in your love.
Amen.

## When Cousins Visit

(to be read by one of the children)

Dear Jesus,
we remember today how much you loved your family
and especially your cousin John the Baptist.
We thank you for the presence our cousin(s), (name/s).
Be with us as we share this meal,
and always keep us close to one another.
Help us also to remember those who are hungry or lonely
and teach us how to reach out to them.
Amen.

# When Grandparents Visit

Dear God,
thank you for this time we share with
(say whatever name you usually use for your grandparents).
Their (his or her) love
reminds us in a special way of your love for us.
As we share this meal together,
help us to grow in love as a family.
May we always be grateful for one another
and draw strength from our love.
We give you thanks for this food
and the nourishment it provides,
through Jesus our Lord.
Amen.

# To Celebrate a Special Achievement

(This prayer can be used to give thanks for a special accomplishment of some member of the family, for example: a good report card, participation in an athletic or artistic event, a new job, a raise, or an award of some kind.)

Dear God,
we are especially grateful today
for (say what the special achievement is).
We thank you for the many gifts you
have given to (name)
which have helped him/her to do this.
As we share this meal in celebration,
help us to remember all the gifts
you have given to each of us.
Help us to use our gifts for others,
especially those in need.
Bless this food
and continue to
bless (name) with your love.
Amen.

*Special Days*

# First Day of School

O God, today we begin a new year of school.
We thank you for all the fun we had during our time off
and we ask you to be with us in the days ahead.
Send your Holy Spirit upon us
to fill us with enthusiasm for learning and to calm our fears.
Bless our friends, old and new,
and especially our teacher(s), (name/s).
Bless this food before us.
May it strengthen our hearts and minds to grow in your love.
We ask this in Jesus' name.
Amen.

# Last Day of School

Dear Lord,
as we come to the end of this school year
we thank you for everything that has been a part of it:
for all we have learned, for the friends we have made,
and for our teachers and the many other people
who helped us in school.
We thank you for the happy times when we did well
and we thank you for being with us
during the hard times when we struggled.
Bless this food which we share together
and bless the days of vacation that are ahead.
We pray this in Jesus' name.
Amen.

# Mother's Day

O God our Mother,
we thank you for giving us Mom
and for the many ways she shows us your motherly love.
On this her special day we ask you
to bless her with your joy and peace.
As she cares for all of us,
help her to find strength for the many challenges she faces.
Remind us to show our gratitude for all she does,
and especially for who she is.
Bless this meal which we share in celebration of Mom,
and be with all mothers and grandmothers on this day.
Amen.

# Father's Day

O God our Father,
we thank you for giving us Dad
and for the many ways he shows us your fatherly care.
On this his special day
we ask you to bless him with your peace and joy.
Give him the strength and the understanding
that he needs to care for us as a family.
Help us to appreciate more all he does for us
and to show him how much we love him.
Bless this meal which we share to celebrate Dad
and be with all fathers and grandfathers on this day.
Amen.

# First Communion

All loving God,
you created (name) in your image
and gave him/her the gift of life in our family.
Through baptism you welcomed (name)
into your family, the church,
and called him/her to live as your son/daughter.
We thank you for this day,
on which, for the first time, (name) received
your Son Jesus in the eucharist.
May we always be nourished by your presence
so as to grow in friendship with you.
As we continue our celebration around this table,
bless our food
and help us to recognize Christ in one another.
We ask this in Jesus' name.
Amen.

# Confirmation

God our Creator,
from the beginning of time
your Spirit has been at work in our world,
creating, renewing, and transforming all things.
We thank you today for the gift of your Spirit
which (name) has received in the sacrament of confirmation.
May the Holy Spirit continue
to help (name) grow strong in faith and in love,
and guide him/her in all the difficult decisions
he/she will make in the future.
Bless this meal and through our sharing
renew us all with the Spirit's many gifts.
We ask this through Christ our Lord.
Amen.

# First Day of Spring

God of new life,
we give you praise and thanks
for this first day of spring.
We thank you for sustaining us through the winter,
and for the returning warmth of the sun.
We praise you for the new life
which springs from the earth,
for food which nourishes our bodies,
and for the flowers which gladden our hearts.
Bless this meal which we share.
May we too be signs of new life
and hope for our world.
Amen.

# First Day of Summer

God of light and love,
we thank you for this season of summer,
a time of warmth, of growth, and of fun.
May the brightness of the sun remind us of your love.
May the coolness of the waters renew us in your care.
As we rejoice in this season,
help us to be grateful for all your gifts,
especially the food on our table.
Make us mindful too of those who are hungry,
and teach us how to care for them.
We ask this through Jesus,
our light and our Lord.
Amen.

# First Day of Autumn

Bountiful God,
as the season of fall begins, we are grateful
for the rich harvest of the earth:
for corn and wheat,
for apples and peaches,
for fish and fowl.
As the days grow shorter
and the nights turn colder
we rely on your love
to warm us and sustain us.
As we are grateful for your gifts
make us mindful of others
and generous with what we have.
Bless this meal which we share
in the name of Jesus the Lord.
Amen.

LET'S SAY GRACE

# First Day of Winter

O God our Refuge,
on this first day of winter
we give you thanks for our home
and the warmth and shelter it provides for us.
During these shortest days of the year
we remember that your love is always with us,
even in times of cold and darkness.
As you sustained Mary and Joseph on their journey to
Bethlehem,
be with us as we look forward to the celebration of Christmas.
Help us to remember all those in need of food and shelter
and to share with them from the many gifts you give us.
Thank you for this meal
and for all the blessings of this joyful season.
Amen.

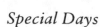

# ADVENT

# First Sunday

Leader: Come Lord Jesus, set us free.
All:       Come Lord Jesus, come.
             (Light the first Advent candle.)

Thank you Lord for this season of Advent
when we prepare for your arrival.
Help us to keep our eyes open
to see you when you come to us.
Bless this food which reminds us of the banquet
we will all share with you one day in heaven. Amen.

Leader: Come Lord Jesus, set us free.
All:       Come Lord Jesus, come.

## Weekdays of the First Week

Leader: Come Lord Jesus, bless this food.
All:       Come Lord Jesus, come.
             (Light the first Advent candle.)

Lord, as we begin to get ready for Christmas
help us to be grateful for all your gifts,
especially the gift of this meal we share together. Amen.

Leader: Come Lord Jesus, bless this food.
All:       Come Lord Jesus, come.

# Second Sunday

Leader: Prepare the way of the Lord,
All:     Make straight his paths.
          (Light two candles.)

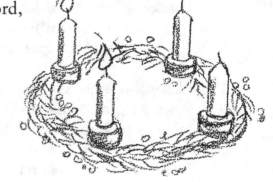

Lord, during this Advent,
help us to prepare your way
by being kind and considerate,
by not thinking of ourselves first,
but of each other's needs.
Thank you for this food which gives us strength. Amen.

Leader: Prepare the way of the Lord,
All:     Make straight his paths.

# Weekdays of the Second Week

Leader: Come Lord Jesus, prepare our hearts.
All:     Come Lord Jesus, come.
          (Light two candles.)

Loving God,
you gave the prophet Isaiah a vision of peace,
where the wolf is a guest of the lamb
and the lion and calf graze together.
May this meal strengthen us to prepare our hearts for you

by making peace with each other
and all the creatures of this earth.
Bless this food we share
and bless us in Jesus' name. Amen.

Leader:  Come Lord Jesus, prepare our hearts.
All:      Come Lord Jesus, come.

# Third Sunday

Leader:  Let us rejoice in the Lord always.
All:      For God has done great things for us.
          (Light three candles, including the pink one.)

Lord, as we share this meal,
fill us with the happiness that comes
from being kind and generous
and from serving you.
Thank you for this time together. Amen.

Leader:  Let us rejoice in the Lord always.
All:      For God has done great things for us.

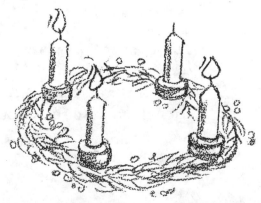

*Advent*

# Weekdays of the Third Week

Leader: Come Lord Jesus, give us joy.
All:      Come Lord Jesus, come.
        (Light three candles, including the pink one.)

Dear Jesus,
we are truly happy that your birthday is near.
Help us to prepare for your coming
by responding to the call of John the Baptist
to be unselfish and patient with one another.
As we share this food,
teach us to share our hearts as well. Amen.

Leader: Come Lord Jesus, give us joy.
All:      Come Lord Jesus, come.

# Fourth Sunday

Leader: Hail Mary full of grace.
All:      The Lord is with you.
        (Light four candles.)

Lord, as the days grow shorter,
we remember that the day of your birth is near.
May the food and the love that we share around this table
strengthen us to share your light with all those we meet. Amen.

Leader:   Hail Mary full of grace.
All:         The Lord is with you.

# Weekdays of the Fourth Week

Leader:  Come Lord Jesus, be our light.
All:         Come Lord Jesus, come.
             (Light four candles.)

Dear God,
thank you for the gift of Mary
who said yes when you asked her
to become the mother of Jesus.
Help us to welcome
him into our hearts
and into our family
as he comes to us this Christmas
and as he is with us now
as we share this meal. Amen.

Leader:  Come Lord Jesus, be our light.
All:         Come Lord Jesus, come.

# CHRISTMAS
## SEASON

# Christmas Eve

Dear God,
as we gather together as a family (and with our friends)
on this special night,
we remember how Mary and Joseph
came to Bethlehem seeking shelter,
but found no place to stay.
As we begin our celebration of Jesus' birth,
help us, by our kindness and generosity,
to welcome him into our home.
Show us how to care for him
by caring for all those in need.
Bless this meal and our celebration this night.
Amen.

# Christmas Day

Loving Father,
on this special day we thank you
for the gift of your Son Jesus
who was born in our world as a helpless baby.
We thank you for one another,
for the love we share,
and the gifts we have exchanged
as signs of that love.
We remember those whom we love who are not with us today,
and ask you to bless us all.
We give you thanks
for this wonderful meal before us.
Make us generous and caring to all those in need.
Amen.

# The Days After Christmas

Gracious God,
we thank you for this joyful season,
for the warmth of family and friends,
and for the many gifts we have received from your goodness.
Bless this meal and each of us who shares it.
Amen.

# Sunday After Christmas

## (Holy Family)

Thank you Lord for the gift of our family.
Help us to support one another by our love,
to encourage one another by our compliments.
Help us to forgive the hurts caused by our forgetfulness.
Bless this food
and all who are gathered at our table.
Amen.

# New Year's Eve

Generous God,
as we look back on this past year
we remember the people, the places, and the events
that were a part of our lives.
We recall that there were difficult times and good times.
And we know that through all the days,
even when we did not realize it,
you were with us.
We thank you for your loving presence
and ask you to be with us once again
as we share this meal together.
Amen.

# New Year's Day

## (Mary, Mother of God)

God of all hopefulness,
As we begin this new year
we ask for the presence of your Holy Spirit
to guide and protect us.
We pray for good health in our family
and peace in our world.
And we thank you for the gift of your mother, Mary,
and the many other blessings you give us,
especially for this food.
Amen.

LET'S SAY GRACE

# Epiphany

## (Sunday after New Year's Day)

All loving God,
today we remember how you sent a bright star
to guide the wise men to Jesus. As a sign of their love,
they offered him gifts of gold, frankincense, and myrrh.
Help us to follow our guiding stars
as they lead us to you.
May this meal strengthen us on our journey
and bring us closer together in love.
Amen.

# Baptism of the Lord

## (Sunday after the Epiphany)

Faithful God,
we remember today the baptism of your Son Jesus
and the words that you spoke as your Spirit descended upon him:
"You are my beloved Son, on you my favor rests."
As you filled Jesus with energy and courage
to carry out your work in this world, give us your Spirit's power
to live as signs of your presence
in our family, in our schools, and in our work.
May this meal be a source of strength and life,
and may the richness of our table
remind us to care for all your beloved daughters and sons.
We pray in Jesus' name.
Amen.

# LENT

# Ash Wednesday

God of mercy,
as we begin the season of Lent today,
we wear ashes to remember our sins
and we turn to you for forgiveness.
Help us not to think so much about ourselves
but about others and you.
During these forty days help us
to pray more,
to keep our promises,
to make sacrifices,
and to share with those in need.
And bless this food we share.
Amen.

# 🌶 Lent Weekdays 🌶

## Monday

Lord Jesus,
you always reached out to those who sinned.
You drank water with the Samaritan woman
and shared bread with Zacchaeus the tax collector.
Be with us now at this table.
Help us to turn away from sin
and be faithful to your gospel.
Amen.

## Tuesday

Loving God,
as we gather for this meal
we remember those who are hungry,
those who are homeless,
and those who are sick.
During this season of Lent
help us always to find new ways to
care for them, and to share from what we have.
We thank you for this food.
Amen.

LET'S SAY GRACE

# Wednesday

Lord Jesus,
you are the Living Water,
you are the Bread of Life
you are the Light of the World.
May the food and the love
we share at this meal
strengthen us to
give water to the thirsty,
bread to the hungry,
and light to those in darkness.
Amen.

# Thursday

Lord God,
may everything we do
during this season of Lent
begin with your inspiration,
carry on with your help,
and reach its conclusion under your guidance.
Bless this meal we share
and teach us to be grateful for all your gifts.
Amen.

# Friday

Blessed are you God of our ancestors,
for forty years you fed your people
with manna and quail as they wandered through the desert.
Sustain us in our fasting and sacrifice
during these forty days of Lent
so that we may come at last to the joy of Easter.
We ask this in your name.
Amen.

# ❧ LENT SUNDAYS ❧

# First Sunday

Dear Jesus,
you fasted for forty days and forty nights
and afterward you were hungry.
During this season of Lent,
help us to imitate you,
to give up something so that we can think more of others.
We are grateful for all you have given us,
especially for this meal.
Amen.

# Second Sunday

Lord Jesus Christ,
we remember today how you brought your friends
Peter, James, and John to the top of a high mountain
where your clothes were as bright as any light
and your face dazzled like the sun.
"How good it is to be here," Peter said.
During this time of Lent,
help us to grow in friendship with you.
Fill our hearts with the brightness of your love,
so that we can serve one another
and appreciate how truly good it is to be with you.
Amen.

# Third Sunday

Jesus, we remember today
how you came to the well in Samaria feeling hungry and thirsty.
When you asked the woman for a drink
she not only gave you water, but also her heart.
As we come to this table, we too are hungry and thirsty.
We ask you to nourish our bodies and our hearts
so that during this Lent we can grow in your love.
Amen.

# Fourth Sunday

Merciful God,
today we remember the story of the Prodigal Son.
Like the forgiving father,
you set a wonderful banquet before us
when we turn from our sins and come home to you.
As we share this meal
help us to remember those we need to forgive.
We thank you for this food
and for the gift of our family.
Amen.

# Fifth Sunday

Lord Jesus,
you taught us that before a grain of wheat
can grow and produce much fruit,
it must die.
As we see this food before us
we remember that it has sprung from many seeds
that died to give new life.
Help us to remember that we are all like seeds:
our selfishness must die
so that we can grow in love.
Thank you for this food we share.
Amen.

# Passion (Palm) Sunday

Leader: Blessed is the one who comes in the name of the Lord.
All:        Hosanna in the highest.

Lord Jesus,
although you were a king, you rode on a donkey.
The people praised you with their voices,
but did not follow your word with their actions.
As we begin this Holy Week,
help us to praise you not only in our words
but also in our deeds.
Strengthen us through this meal we now share.

Leader: Blessed is the one who comes
             in the name of the Lord.
All:        Hosanna in the highest.

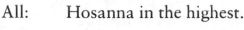

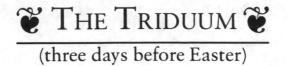

# ❦ THE TRIDUUM ❦
## (three days before Easter)

## Holy Thursday

Dear Jesus,
today we remember
how you shared your last supper with your friends.
You gave them bread and wine saying,
"This is my body. This is my blood."
And after dinner you washed their feet.
We thank you for the gift of your presence in the eucharist
and for teaching us how to care for one another.
As we share this meal,
help us to remember to imitate your generous love
by giving from our hearts to all who are in need.
Amen.

# Good Friday

Lord Jesus Christ,
on this most holy day you gave your life on the cross
to show us how much you love us.
In the midst of your suffering
you forgave those who were crucifying you
and you placed your life in your Father's hands.
As we share this simple meal
we remember your love.
We ask you to help us grow in forgiveness and trust,
and to recognize you in all those who are suffering today.
Amen.

# Holy Saturday

## (Easter Vigil)

Lord Jesus,
when you died on the cross,
your friends and followers were saddened and shocked.
But three days later,
God raised you up to new life and they rejoiced.
As we prepare to celebrate Easter,
help us to remember its true meaning in our lives
May we never give up hope
and rejoice always in your presence with us.
Bless this meal which we share together.
Amen.

*Lent*

# EASTER
## SEASON

# Easter and the Sundays of the Easter Season

Leader: Jesus Christ is risen today.
All:      Alleluia.
Leader: We rejoice and are glad.
All:      Alleluia.

Lord Jesus,
we celebrate your resurrection
and we rejoice in your love.
You are with us now as we share this meal
offering us forgiveness, peace, and new life.
Help us to recognize you in the breaking of this bread,
and strengthen us to share
the good news of your rising with others.

Leader: Jesus Christ is risen today.
All:      Alleluia.
Leader: We rejoice and are glad.
All:      Alleluia.

*Easter Season*

# ❧ Easter Weekdays ❧

Lord Jesus, you are the Bread of Life,
the Living Water,
the Good Shepherd
who prepares a banquet for us
and fills our cups to overflowing.
May this meal nourish our bodies
and may your presence among us renew our spirits.
Strengthen us to serve you in each other,
especially in those without hope.
We ask this in faith.
Amen.

## Ascension Thursday

Jesus, risen Lord,
as you ascended into heaven
you said to your disciples,
"Look, I am with you always; yes, to the end of time."
Be with us as we seek
to share your love with all those we meet,
and be present at our table
to strengthen and renew us.
May this meal be a sign
of our love for one another
and help us to follow your call.
Amen.

# Pentecost

Leader: Come, Holy Spirit,
All:     Renew the hearts of your people.

Gracious God,
you first sent the Holy Spirit
upon the frightened disciples at Pentecost
to renew their faith
and strengthen their courage
to preach the gospel of your Son Jesus.
As we share this meal together,
send your Spirit upon us to
renew us in faith
and strengthen us to share the good news
with all we meet.

Leader: Come, Holy Spirit,
All:     Renew the hearts of your people.

# HOLY DAYS

## AND HOLIDAYS

# January 4
# Elizabeth Anne Seton

Elizabeth Anne Seton is the first native-born American saint. A mother of five children, her husband died when she was twenty-seven years old. She converted to Catholicism and began a religious order called the Sisters of Charity of St. Joseph. She founded a number of schools in Maryland and also worked with orphans and the sick.

Loving God,
we remember today the life
of St. Elizabeth Anne Seton,
a mother, a teacher,
and a compassionate friend
to orphans and the sick.
As we share this meal together,
help us to remember and be grateful
for all those who care for us,
especially our teachers.
As we return to school
after Christmas vacation,
make us aware of the gifts
we have to share with others:
the gift of knowledge, the gift of friendship,
and the gift of helping hands to those in need.
We ask you to bless this food in Jesus' name.
Amen.

*Holy Days and Holidays*

# Third Monday of January
# Martin Luther King Day

This great leader of the civil rights movement was born on January 15, 1929 in Atlanta, Georgia. Like his father and grandfather, he was a minister and an eloquent preacher. Martin Luther King, Jr. came to national attention in December of 1955 when he organized a boycott of the Montgomery, Alabama bus system after Rosa Parks was jailed for refusing to give up her seat to a white man. He is perhaps best remembered for his "I Have a Dream" speech, given before 250,000 people who gathered in August 1963 near the Washington Monument to demonstrate for equal rights for all Americans. On April 4, 1968 Martin Luther King was assassinated in Memphis, Tennessee, a victim of the hatred he had spoken so forcefully against.

O God of justice,
you raised up Martin Luther King
as a voice crying in the wilderness
for peace and harmony among all races and creeds.
Help us to dream his dream of freedom and equality.
Help us to remove all prejudice in ourselves
and to right the wrongs caused
by ignorance and fear.
Teach us how to share our bread
with those who are oppressed,
and bless this food
which we share in your name.
Amen.

# January 25
# Conversion of St. Paul

Before he became a believer, Paul was a fierce persecutor of the church, feared by Christians everywhere. He even stood by and approved as St. Stephen, the first martyr, was stoned to death. One day, as he was riding his horse on a journey, Jesus appeared to Paul and asked, "Why do you persecute me?" Paul not only became a Christian after this incident, but also travelled throughout the world preaching the good news to Jews and Gentiles alike. The story of Paul's conversion and his missionary efforts are found in the Acts of the Apostles.

Today, January 25, also marks the end of a week of prayer for Christian unity.

Lord Jesus Christ,
the bright light of your presence
changed the fear and hatred in Paul's heart
to love and compassion.
May the same light
be with us at this table.
Let it calm our fears
and mend the wounds that divide us
as a family and as members of the body of Christ.
May this food strengthen us
to the signs of your presence
in our words and deeds.
Amen.

# Sunday in Late January
## Super Bowl Sunday

The Super Bowl for the pro football championship was first played in January 1967 in Los Angeles. That game pitted the Green Bay Packers against the Kansas City Chiefs. The Packers won. Though not an officially recognized holiday, many Americans gather together on Super Bowl Sunday with family, friends, and neighbors to share a meal before or during the game.

Almighty God,
you give us this day of rest and relaxation,
this time to enjoy the Super Bowl together.
We thank you for all your gifts,
and for this good food which we share.
As you have blessed these athletes with strength and agility,
give us the energy and wisdom we need
to be faithful to the calling
you have given each of us.
We ask this through Christ our Lord.
Amen.

# Late January or Early February
## Chinese New Year

The date of the Chinese New Year is determined according to a lunar calendar, and so varies from year to year. The Chinese divide the years into cycles of twelve, with each year being named for an animal. The new year is celebrated with festive meals and with parades and fireworks.

God of all people,
as we remember Chinese New Year
help us to be aware that all people,
of every race, language, and country
are your children.
Help us to appreciate the differences
among us and learn from each other.
Show us your face
in the smiles and laughter
of children everywhere.
Thank you for this meal
and for this special day.
Amen.

*Holy Days and Holidays*

# February 2
## The Presentation of the Lord

Today we remember how Joseph and Mary brought Jesus to the Temple in Jerusalem forty days after his birth and presented him to the Jewish priests. Luke 2:22-38 describes how Joseph and Mary made the customary offering of the poor—two turtle doves—and then heard the prophetic words of Simeon and Anna.

February 2 is also the midpoint between the first day of winter and the first day of spring. For this reason, numerous popular customs have grown up around this day. Traditionally, it was a day for blessing candles, whose light illuminates the winter nights. And, as everyone knows, it is Groundhog Day. We watch to see if the groundhog sees its shadow and find out how many more days of winter there will be.

God of all hopefulness,
you sent the infant Jesus
as a light shining in the darkness
to fulfill the longings of your people.
As we rejoice in his coming,
we look for the light of his presence in our lives
and the warmth of his love in our home.
May this meal we share renew us in the midst of winter.
May it strengthen us to hasten
the coming of your reign.
Amen.

# February 14
## Valentine's Day

The name of this holiday comes from St. Valentine, a priest who was martyred by the Roman emperor Claudius II around the year 269. Tradition holds that on this day in mild climates around the Mediterranean Sea, birds often begin to choose their mates. The custom of sending valentine love notes on February 14 began in medieval times.

God of love,
we thank you for all the people who
love and care for us,
especially our families.
Help us to show our love in return.
May the valentines we share today
be signs of our sincere care and friendship
for those who receive them.
We ask you to bless this food
and to be with those who may
feel lonely or forgotten today.
Amen.

# Third Monday of February
## Presidents' Day

Today we celebrate two of our nation's greatest presidents, George Washington and Abraham Lincoln.

George Washington was born on February 23, 1732 in Virginia. He was the general of the colonial army during the Revolutionary War. On April 20, 1789 he became the first president of the United States. As he took the oath of office, he recited from Psalm 127: "Unless the Lord build the house, they labor in vain who build it."

Abraham Lincoln was born on February 12, 1804 in Kentucky. As the sixteenth president of the United States, Lincoln sought to preserve the union during the Civil War. In 1863 he issued the Emancipation Proclamation to free all slaves. He was assassinated on April 14, 1865 at the Ford Theater in Washington, D.C.

God of justice,
you inspired George Washington and Abraham Lincoln
to help create a nation where all men and women,
regardless of race or religion,
could live in freedom and equality.
Help us to remember their ideals
and to root our own efforts in your justice.
Bless this meal, and through it give us strength
to work for what is right and fair.
Amen.

# March 17
## St. Patrick's Day

St. Patrick is the patron saint of Ireland and is special to all people of Irish descent. He was born around the year 389 in England and first came to Ireland at about the age of sixteen, when he was carried there as a slave by pirates. After six years he escaped, but soon heard the call of God to go back to Ireland as a missionary. After being ordained a bishop he returned to Ireland where he converted the Celtic chiefs and people throughout the land.

Christ be with us,
be within us.
Christ beside us,
behind and before us.
Christ comfort us,
nourish and strengthen us.
Christ is with the hungry,
the weak, and the lonely.
Christ be among us,
feed and send us.

*(based on the Breastplate of St. Patrick)*

# March 19
## Joseph

St. Joseph was the husband of Mary and the foster-father of Jesus. Joseph played a key role in the events of Jesus' birth. Twice he received a message from God in a dream, telling him not to be afraid to take Mary as his wife and then warning him to flee to Egypt to escape Herod's jealous wrath.

Joseph was a carpenter and taught this trade to Jesus. Because he is not mentioned during Jesus' public life, Christians have always believed that he must have died before then. Joseph is especially revered by people of Italian descent who celebrate this day with special foods.

God of love,
you chose St. Joseph to be the foster-father of Jesus,
and through him taught Jesus to call you "Abba" (or Daddy).
We thank you for Joseph's strong faith and constant care.
Help us to grow in faith and love
and to be grateful for all the gifts you give us,
especially for this meal which we bless in Christ's name.
Amen.

# March 25
## The Annunciation

Chapter 1 of St. Luke's gospel tells us how the angel Gabriel announced to Mary that she was to be the mother of the long-awaited Messiah. The angel's words form the first part of the Hail Mary:

Hail Mary, full of grace,
the Lord is with you.
Blessed are you among women.

Mary said in reply, "Let it happen to me as you have said."

Lord God, you sent the angel Gabriel
to announce to Mary
that she would be the
mother of your Son.
Today we remember her
trust in your word
and her faith in
your promise.
As she said yes to you,
help us to do your
will in all things each day.
Bless this meal which we share,
and keep our hearts and minds open to the unexpected ways
that you speak to us through one another.
We ask this through Jesus our Lord.
Amen.

# April 1
## April Fool's Day

Today is a day to play tricks and to try to fool one another. There are many ideas about how this custom began, although no one knows exactly how it got started. One story goes that it was on this day that Noah was fooled by the weather and mistakenly sent out a dove to look for land. April 1 was once was the first day of spring (before the calendar was corrected) and spring is certainly a season when we, like Noah, can find that the weather plays tricks on us!

O God our Creator,
we thank you for the joy of this spring season,
and for the many fun times we share together.
Help us to make each other happy,
to laugh, to smile, and to play together.
Bless this food.
Make this and every meal
a time to rejoice in your love.
Amen.

# April 22
## Earth Day

Earth Day is a time when we grow in our awareness of the fragile state of the environment and work to find solutions for preserving it. For those in the northern hemisphere, Earth Day comes at a time when spring is entering its fullness. Earth Day is a good day to express our thankfulness for land, air, and water, and to renew our commitment to preserve these gifts of God for the future.

God of all creation,
as the life of spring grows all around us
we give you thanks for the beauty of our world,
for sun and rain,
for flowers and crops.
As we share in the bounty of the land,
help us to grow in respect for the earth
and to preserve its resources for all people.
Bless this food we share,
a gift of your love
and fruits of your creation.
Amen.

# April 25
# Mark

Although St. Mark's gospel is arranged second in the New Testament, scholars believe that it was actually the first gospel to be written. Mark was a companion of Peter and his gospel probably reflects what Peter taught him about the life and teachings of Jesus. His gospel emphasizes Jesus' suffering and calls us to follow Jesus, even when it is difficult. The Acts of the Apostles also tell us that Mark travelled with Paul and Barnabas as a missionary.

Gracious God,
through the Holy Spirit
you inspired St. Mark to write the first gospel.
We thank you for the gift of your word
which teaches and nourishes us.
As you feed our spirits through the scriptures,
strengthen our bodies with this food.
May your Spirit inspire us
to share the good news with others.
Amen.

# May 1
## Joseph the Worker

Today is the midpoint of spring, when the beauty and life of the season are in full bloom. Through the centuries May 1 has been celebrated as a day of new life, a joyful day to affirm the gifts of love and work. Our Christian calendar reminds us of St. Joseph, whose love and work sustained Mary and Jesus.

Bountiful God,
we thank you for all your gifts:
for the gift of spring,
with its warmth, light, and flowers;
for the gift of work,
which challenges, supports, and fulfills us;
and for the gift of love,
with its kindness, patience, and forgiveness.
Bless this meal which we now share,
a gift from your bounty,
a reward for our labors,
and a sign of your love.
Amen.

# May 5
## Cinco de Mayo

The fifth of May—Cinco de Mayo—is a national holiday in Mexico and is commemorated as a day of pride by Mexican-Americans throughout the United States. On May 5, 1862 a smaller Mexican force defeated an invading French army at the Battle of Puebla. This event is celebrated as an occasion of honor and freedom.

God of power and mercy,
as we pray for and with the people of Mexico,
we thank you for the gift of freedom.
We thank you for this day of fiesta
and for the gift of this food.
We remember all those who are hungry
as well as those who are not free.
Show us the way to bring your love to all people.
We ask this in Jesus' name.
Amen.

# May 31
## The Visitation

We remember today how Mary, a very young woman in the first month of her pregnancy, made a long and difficult journey from Nazareth to the hill country of Judea to be with her cousin, Elizabeth, who was also pregnant. Mary came to offer Elizabeth help and support and to share with her the news that Mary had received from the angel Gabriel. When she arrived, Mary proclaimed the beautiful prayer we call the Magnificat.

Our souls proclaim your greatness, O God,
and our spirits rejoice in you, our Savior.
For you have done great things for us,
and holy is your name.
You turn away the proud and the selfish,
but you raise up the lowly and the poor.
Teach us to be grateful for all your gifts,
and to follow Mary's example of thoughtfulness to others.
Bless this meal, and make our lives holy,
through Jesus, the son of Mary and our brother.
Amen.

*(based on Luke 1:46-55)*

# Last Monday of May
## Memorial Day

On Memorial Day we remember all those who have died in the many wars our nation has fought. This day was once called Decoration Day because of the custom of decorating the graves of soldiers, a practice that began after the Civil War. Today many families visit the graves of loved ones and remember them in prayer.

God of peace,
we recall today the words of Jesus,
"Blessed are the peacemakers,
they shall be called the sons and daughters of God."
As we remember all who have died because of war,
inspire the leaders of all nations
to turn away from war and work for peace.
Help us also to live in peace with one another,
and with peoples of every nation, race, and creed.
Bless this food we share
as we celebrate this day with our family and friends.
Amen.

# June 24
# The Birth of John the Baptist

Although we do not know the actual day of John's birth, St. Luke's gospel tells us that after the annunciation Mary went to visit Elizabeth, John's mother, who was in her sixth month of pregnancy. Since the annunciation is celebrated on March 25, John's birthday comes three months later on June 24.

John the Baptist's birthday is almost six months opposite from Christmas and very close to the first day of summer. Just as John once said of Jesus: "He must increase, I must decrease," Christians have noted how after the birthday of John the Baptist the days begin to grow shorter, while after Jesus' birthday they grow longer.

God of our ancestors,
you called John while still in his mother's womb
to announce the coming of Jesus.
As we begin this season of summer,
make us aware of the many chances in the days ahead
to be signs of your love.
We thank you for this meal,
and for the opportunity it gives us
to serve and care for each other.
Amen.

# June 27
# Helen Keller

Helen Keller was born on this date in 1880 in Tuscumbia, Alabama. Due to a severe illness at the age of nineteen months, she became blind and deaf. A short time later she lost her ability to speak. When she was almost seven years old her parents found a wonderful teacher for her named Anne Mansfield Sullivan. With her teacher's help Helen began to speak after just one month. Eventually she learned to read Braille and to write as well. Helen Keller went on to school and eventually attended college. She wrote many books about her life and her struggle to achieve, despite her disabilities.

Dear God,
thank you for the gifts of sight, hearing, and speech.
Help us not to take them for granted
and to use all the gifts you give us to help others.
And help us also to remember,
that when bodies are not so agile
or minds are not so quick,
that each of us nevertheless has special gifts
to share with one another.
We give you thanks for the gift of this food
and for all the talents and abilities we have received
through your generous love.
Amen.

# June 29
# Peter and Paul

It is an ancient tradition to celebrate together the feast of these two apostles. Although in many ways their lives were quite different, there are some interesting parallels between them. Both were great leaders in the early church: Peter as the leader of the apostles and Paul as a great missionary. Both were given new names by Jesus as a sign of their new mission. Jesus changed Simon's name to Peter, meaning "rock," and Saul's name to Paul, to signify his new mission to the Gentiles. And both were eventually put to death in Rome for their faith.

Lord Jesus,
you called Peter and Paul
to share their faith and love for you with the whole world.
You gave them new names and led them to do things
beyond what they could ever have imagined.
Just as you strengthened them by your presence
through word and eucharist,
be with us during this meal
to renew our faith and love.
Help us, like Peter, to put our faith in you.
Help us, like Paul, to make love our greatest gift.
Bless this food and the friendship we share.
Amen.

# July 4
# Independence Day

On July 4, 1776 the Continental Congress issued the Declaration of Independence. Written mostly by Thomas Jefferson, it declared the thirteen American colonies to be free and independent states, no longer subject to the king of England. Although the Revolutionary War had already begun, this was the official birth of the United States of America.

O God our Creator,
with the founders of our country,
we believe that you have given all people
"certain inalienable rights . . . among these life, liberty,
and the pursuit of happiness."
We thank you for our country,
for the freedom and opportunity it gives us,
and for its beauty and bounty.
As we celebrate with this meal
we ask you to bless our food and to bless our nation.
Help us to choose leaders inspired by its ideals
and mindful of the rights of all people.
Help us to use our nation's gifts wisely,
and to extend your care to the needy of the world.
We ask this through Christ our Lord.
Amen.

# July 14
## Kateri Tekakwitha

The daughter of an Algonquin mother and a Mohawk father, Kateri was born in the mountains of central New York near the village of Auriesville in 1656. This was the place where, just nine years earlier, two French priests were tortured to death by the Huron and Iroquois Indians. When she was four-years-old, Kateri's parents and brothers died of smallpox. She was left scarred and half-blind by the disease. She then lived with her uncle, the tribal chief.

Attracted by the preaching of the missionaries, Kateri became a Christian at the age of nineteen, even though her new religion made her an outcast in her tribe. One night she left her people and made a two-hundred-mile journey on foot to a village near Montreal. There she lived with an older Iroquois woman, dedicating herself to prayer and Christian service.

God of mercy,
you filled Kateri with so much love for you
that she gladly followed your call
without counting the cost.
Give us that same love too,
so that we can grow each day as your daughters and sons.
Bless this meal that we share
and help us, like the native peoples of North America,
to grow in reverence and appreciation
for all your gifts.
Amen.

# July 22
# Mary Magdalene

Before she met Jesus, Mary Magdalene was known as a terrible sinner, but after her conversion she became one of his most dedicated followers. At the crucifixion most of the apostles ran away, but Mary was one of a few women who stood faithfully at the foot of Jesus' cross. She was also one of the three women who came to anoint his body on Easter morning and ultimately discovered the empty tomb. As she stood weeping outside the tomb she saw a man she thought was a gardener. When she asked where they had taken the body of Jesus, the man spoke her name. She then recognized that he was indeed Jesus.

Faithful God,
you transformed the life of Mary Magdalene by your love for her.
You gave her the courage
to abandon her old way of life to follow Jesus,
and the devotion to stand by him
through the agony of the cross.
You chose her as the first witness of the resurrection
and sent her to proclaim the good news.
Help us to imitate Mary and to grow in love for Jesus.
Through this meal which we share in Jesus' name,
help us to recognize Christ in one another
and fill us with the joy of his presence.
Amen.

# July 26
# Joachim and Ann

Although we do not know anything about their lives, and cannot even be certain of their names, we remember Joachim and Ann as the parents of Mary. From what we know of their daughter we can assume that they too were holy people. They, along with Joseph's parents, would have arranged their daughter's wedding; and Mary would have been living in their home at the time of the annunciation. We can only guess about their reaction to this news, as well as what role they played in the raising of their grandson, Jesus.

Gentle God,
we thank you for the gift of parents and grandparents
who love and care for us throughout our lives.
As we remember Joachim and Ann,
the parents of Mary and the grandparents of Jesus,
we ask you to help us appreciate
all that we have received from our families.
As you were present in their home and at their table,
be here with us.
Nourish us with your grace
and fill us with compassion for all those in need.
Amen.

# July 29
# Martha

Martha lived with her sister Mary and her brother Lazarus in the village of Bethany, a short distance from Jerusalem. Jesus was their friend and he often stayed at their home. One time Martha complained to Jesus that Mary spent to much time talking with him and not enough time working. Jesus told her that in talking and listening to him rather than only doing household chores, Mary had made the better choice.

When their brother Lazarus died, it took Jesus four days to reach the sisters. When Martha heard that Jesus was near, she ran out to meet him and said, "Lord, if you had been here, my brother would not have died." In response to her faith, Jesus raised Lazarus back to life.

Lord Jesus,
we remember today that you shared many meals
with your friends Martha, Mary, and Lazarus.
You laughed and cried with them.
You settled their arguments and took away their sorrow.
May your quiet presence at our table
bring us the same happiness and peace.
Bless our food and be with us always,
in times of trouble and in times of joy.
Amen.

# August 6
# The Transfiguration

Today we remember how Jesus took Peter, James, and John to the top of a mountain. There, as the gospel of St. Matthew tells us, "his face shone like the sun and his clothes became as dazzling as light." Moses and Elijah appeared with Jesus. Although Peter was frightened, he said, "Lord it is wonderful for us to be here," and offered to build three shelters in honor of the occasion. Just then the voice of God was heard, "This is my Son, the beloved. Listen to him."

Holy God,
you gave us your Son Jesus
to show us your love and to
guide us to you.
We thank you for the times
when we have seen his face
in our friends,
in those who are hungry,
in those who are sad,
in those who are joyful.
As we gather around this table we say with Peter,
"Lord, it is wonderful for us to be here."
Bless our food and our conversation.
Teach us to listen to one another
and help us always to listen to you.
We ask this in Jesus' name.
Amen.

*Holy Days and Holidays*

# August 11
## Clare of Assisi

Clare was born in the Italian town of Assisi in 1194, thirteen years after St. Francis. At the age of eighteen she ran away from her wealthy family to follow Francis. After a few years she became the leader of the first community of Franciscan sisters at San Damiano. There she lived a life of prayer and community until her death in 1253.

Gracious God,
you filled St. Clare with so much love
that she longed to spend her life
in prayer and service to others.
You gave her the courage to leave behind
a life of comfort and security
for an unknown and uncertain future.
Fill us with the same love for you and for others.
And, as you gave Clare and Francis the gift of friendship,
give us friends to support and guide us.
Bless this food, bless us, and bless all of our friends.
Amen.

# August 15
## The Assumption

Although the Bible does not tell us anything about Mary's life after the day of Pentecost, Christian tradition holds that Mary spent the last years of her life with the apostle John in Ephesus, a town in present-day Turkey. A church in Jerusalem—the Church of the Dormition (which means "falling asleep")—marks a place for Mary's death.

Since the fifth century Christians have celebrated a feast of the Assumption that is based on the belief that Mary was taken up into heaven "body and soul." Christians believe that Mary now enjoys the fullness of salvation that we will all share in at the time of the final resurrection of the dead.

Ever-living God,
you called Mary to be the mother of your Son, Jesus.
When her life of service and witness on earth was completed,
you gave her the fullness of joy in heaven.
As we remember her faith and generous love,
help us to follow her example.
In sharing this meal we look forward to the day
when we will celebrate
a great and joyful banquet at your table in heaven
with Mary,
with the saints,
and with all those we love.
Amen.

# August 27 and 28
## Monica and Augustine

St. Monica and St. Augustine are unique in the Christian calendar because they are mother and son. They came from the city of Tagaste in North Africa. As a brilliant young man Augustine pursued his goal to becoming a teacher. He lived a wild life, caring little for anything but his own pleasure. For a while Monica would not even let him enter her house, but then she had a vision that he would be converted.

She prayed for him constantly and followed him all the way to Milan in Italy. There Augustine experienced an unexpected conversion to Christ. He went on to become a great leader and teacher in the early church. At peace at last, Monica died shortly after her son's conversion.

Faithful God,
you never give up on us,
even when we wander far from you.
Like a devoted mother, you are always there,
always ready to welcome us home.
As we remember the lives of Monica and Augustine,
help us to open our hearts more widely to you
and fill us with gratitude
for these gifts of food
and all of your many gifts.
Amen.

# First Monday in September
## Labor Day

The first holiday to celebrate working people took place in 1882 in New York City. The practice of a "labor day" caught on quickly throughout the United States. In 1894 President Grover Cleveland declared Labor Day to be a national holiday. Today Labor Day also marks the end of the summer-vacation season.

Holy God,
your grace is always at work in our lives.
You labored for six days to create the world.
You sent your Son Jesus among us
to work as a carpenter and to preach the good news.
Your Spirit is always active,
recreating and renewing creation in your love.
We thank you for this day to celebrate our work.
We are grateful for the strength of our bodies,
the skills of our hands, and the knowledge of our minds.
We remember also those who are unemployed or disabled
and ask you to help and guide them.
Thank you for this meal
and all who labored so that we might enjoy it.
Amen.

# September 8
## The Birth of Mary

Although we do not know the exact date of Mary's birth, Christians have celebrated it on this day since the seventh century. From September 8, the date of the feast of the Immaculate Conception, December 8, was determined by counting back nine months from birth to conception. Mary's birthday is one of only three birthdays commemorated on the Christian calendar. Along with the births of Jesus and John the Baptist, Mary's birthday celebrates the dawn of salvation.

God of life and love,
we celebrate today the birth of Mary.
From the first moment of her life you called her by name
and prepared her for the great work
she was to do as the mother of Jesus.
Help us to hear your call each day
and to say yes when you ask us to serve you.
As we share this meal together, help us to be grateful
for all the opportunities you give our family
to care for one another and to reach out to those in need.
Bless this food and bless us all
in Jesus' name.
Amen.

# September 21
# Matthew

St. Matthew was originally a tax collector, and because of that he was hated by his fellow Jews. He worked for the Romans, not only collecting taxes for the occupying government, but keeping some money for himself as well. Nevertheless, when Jesus passed by Matthew's tax office one day and said, "Follow me," Matthew immediately got up, left his post, and followed him. Matthew then gave a dinner for Jesus, inviting other tax collectors and notorious sinners. When some of the Pharisees complained about this, Jesus said, "It is not the healthy who need the doctor, but the sick." Matthew became one of Jesus' apostles and eventually composed the gospel that bears his name.

God of mercy,
you sent Jesus to proclaim your love
to the rich and poor, the good and bad.
Help us to hear Jesus' call
and, like Matthew, follow him.
May we always welcome Jesus to our table,
and recognize his presence
in the faces of those whom others dislike.
Bless this food and teach us to share
your blessings with others.
Amen.

# September 29

# Michael, Gabriel, and Raphael, Archangels

The word angel means "messenger of God." Michael, Gabriel, and Raphael are called archangels—a higher level of angel—as they are the only angels named in the Bible. Michael appears in the Book of Daniel as a great prince who defends Israel against its enemies, and in the Book of Revelation as a warrior who gains victory over the powers of evil. In the Book of Tobit, Raphael is sent to help Tobit's son Tobias on his journeys. And it is Gabriel is who announces to the virgin Mary that she was to give birth to a son who would be the Messiah.

The reform of the church's calendar joined the feasts of these three archangels. Prior to that, September 29 was the feast of St. Michael alone. In England it was called Michaelmas, and marked the beginning of autumn.

Holy God,
your care for us is more than we can imagine,
and your love touches us in so many ways.
As once you sent your archangels Michael, Gabriel, and Raphael
to guide and protect your chosen ones,
let them be our companions, to lead and watch over us.
As we begin the season of autumn
may we celebrate your presence in the beauty of nature,
and be messengers of your love to all who we meet.
Bless this meal we now share, and bless all we do in Jesus' name.
Amen.

# October 1
## Thérèse of Lisieux

St. Thérèse lived about one hundred years ago in France. She entered the Carmelite order at the young age of fifteen and died from illness in 1897 at the age of twenty-four. She is remembered for her patience with others, her desire to do little things to help them, and her ability to accept her illness without complaint.

Dear God,
we thank you today
for the life of St. Thérèse.
Help us to imitate her example
by being patient,
by going out of our way
to help others,
and by accepting difficulties
without complaining.
We thank you for all the little ways
your love comes to us:
in the kindness of others,
in their patience with us,
and in their words of forgiveness.
We thank you for this meal
and for (name) who prepared it.
Amen.

# October 2
## The Guardian Angels

Belief in guardian angels comes from the words of Jesus: "See that you never despise any of these little ones, for I tell you that their angels in heaven are continually in the presence of my Father" (Mt 18:10). The church's night prayer also speaks of angels who watch over us: "He has given his angels orders about you, to guard you wherever you go" (Ps 91:11). Our belief in guardian angels does not mean that we will always be preserved from trouble or harm, but reminds us that God's love is always with us, no matter what happens.

Loving God,
we come together
to share this meal
after a day filled
with many activities.
In our work and our play,
in our travels and in our rest,
your presence is always with us.
You give us the friendship
of our guardian angels
to guide us and guard us,
to remind us of your presence, and to keep us on the right path.
Help us to be aware that your love is ever near,
and to be grateful for all the gifts that we receive
from your generous hand, especially the gift of this meal.
Amen.

LET'S SAY GRACE

# October 4
## Francis of Assisi

As a rich young man, Francis could do basically whatever he wanted. He had all the possessions a person could ever need. But Francis still found his life wanting, and so he did an unusual thing: he gave away everything. He left his friends and family and went off and tried to follow Jesus' way of simplicity and love. As he travelled about preaching and caring for the poor, he was especially aware of the beauty of all of creation. St. Francis attracted many followers who were called Franciscans. He died in 1226.

O God our Creator,
you have made everything—
the sun and the moon,
the land and the sea,
all animals and races of people.
We thank you for the gifts of creation,
and for all that you have given us.
Help us, like Francis,
to respect your world
and to use our gifts to help others.
Bless the people and animals
who live in our house
(you may wish to name them).
And bless this meal
which we share in Jesus' name.
Amen.

*Holy Days and Holidays*

# October 12

## Columbus Day
### (observed on the second Monday of October)

Today we remember the discovery of America by Christopher Columbus. On October 12, 1492, Columbus landed on the island of San Salvador, which is now called the Dominican Republic. Columbus had set out from Spain with three small ships in hopes of finding a new route to India while also proving that the world was round. Columbus's discovery changed history in a way that neither the people of Europe nor the native peoples of the Americas could ever have imagined.

God of all nations,
as we celebrate Columbus Day
we give you thanks for our country, and for all the different people
who have journeyed here from all over the world
to make it such a wonderful place.
As you gave Christopher Columbus the courage
to set sail into the unknown,
give us the courage to be open to what is new and different
in people of other races and cultures,
especially in the people we meet each day.
Bless this food which we are about to share.
We thank you for all your gifts,
most especially for this wonderful land
whose bounty supplies our needs.
We offer you this prayer through Jesus, our Lord.
Amen.

# October 18
# Luke

St. Luke is the author of two books of the New Testament, the gospel named after him and the Acts of the Apostles. He travelled many times with Paul on his missionary journeys, including a trip all the way to Rome. Luke was a convert to Christianity from paganism and was probably also a doctor. His gospel puts special emphasis on Jesus' care for the poor, the role of women in Jesus' life, and the importance of prayer and following the direction of the Holy Spirit.

Generous God
You gave Luke many gifts.
As a writer, a doctor, and a faithful friend,
he put those gifts to good use for the sake of others.
Help us to be aware of the many talents
we have received from you.
May we show our gratitude
by sharing them with others.
We thank you too for this meal.
Teach us how to share all we have received
with those in need.
We ask this in Jesus' name.
Amen.

# October 31
# Halloween

October 31 marks the midpoint of the season of autumn. The days until February 2 are the shortest days of the year. In the Celtic lands, this night marked the beginning of winter. The Celts believed that on the night of October 31 demons, witches, and evil spirits roamed the earth to greet the season of darkness. The Celts believed these creatures could be warded off by offering them sweets, or by dressing in disguise like one of them. This is the origin of our Halloween customs of trick-or-treating and wearing costumes. We call this night All Hallows (Saints) Eve—Halloween—because it is the evening before All Saints' Day.

Thank you God for this special day,
and for the fun we have with our family, friends, and neighbors.
Help us to be grateful to those who are kind to us,
respectful of their property,
and generous in sharing what we receive.
Bless our trick-or-treating
and all the candy we receive.
Bless this meal we now share,
and keep us safe from harm.
May the light in our jack-o-lanterns
remind us of your love
shining through the darkness of this night.
Amen.

LET'S SAY GRACE

# November 1
## All Saints' Day

All Christians are called to be saints. In fact, in the New Testament letters St. Paul often addressed the people he wrote to as "saints." A saint is a friend of God, whether in this life or the next. We are called to live our lives as saints on earth, following the way of Jesus. The path to sainthood is especially well-defined in the Beatitudes, which is part of the church's prayer for this day. As we celebrate All Saints' Day, we remember all those who have gone before us to enjoy eternal life with God, especially those who are not officially canonized.

Holy God,
on this feast of All Saints we remember the words of Jesus:
"Blessed are those who hunger and thirst for uprightness:
they shall have their fill."
As we gather around this table,
we thank you for this meal which satisfies our physical needs.
We pray that you will increase our hunger and thirst
to be one with you.
We pray that one day we may enjoy your banquet in heaven,
together with our family and friends
who have gone before us, and with all your saints.
We ask this through Christ our Lord.
Amen.

# November 2
## All Souls' Day

Praying for the dead in a special way on the day after All Saints' Day is a Christian custom that dates from the tenth century. On November 2 we remember those who have died because we love them and desire their eternal happiness. We ask God to bring all the departed to perfection in the joy of heaven, and we remember fondly our family members and friends who have gone before us.

Jesus, gentle shepherd,
as we gather for this meal,
we remember the many people whom we love
who are no longer with us.
Forgive all their sins
and bring them safely to your side.
As we share this food,
we trust that they may be seated at your heavenly banquet.
In your love, make us all one,
now and forever in your kingdom.
Amen.

# November 11
## Veterans' Day

Today, along with Memorial Day, is a special day for remembering those who have served in the armed forces, especially those who were killed in battle. Until 1954 this day was called Armistice Day to commemorate the signing of the peace treaty to end World War I. Now we remember all veterans on November 11.

Loving God,
we thank you for the times of peace our nation has enjoyed,
and ask you to bring all wars to an end.
We remember today all veterans,
but especially those who have been killed in wars.
We remember, too,
those who are presently serving in the armed forces.
Keep them safe
and bring them home to their families and friends.
Bless this food we share,
and give us a peace rooted in a just sharing
of the world's resources by all people.
We ask this in Jesus' name.
Amen.

# Fourth Thursday in November
## Thanksgiving Day

Sometime in October 1621, about a year after the first Pilgrims landed in New England, the first Thanksgiving celebration took place. It was a three-day feast in gratitude for the harvest, shared by the English settlers of the Plymouth Colony and the Wampanoag tribe of Native Americans. In 1863, in the midst of the Civil War, President Abraham Lincoln declared the last Thursday in November as a day to give thanks. In 1941 Congress ruled that Thanksgiving Day would be celebrated on the fourth Thursday in November, when it is celebrated today.

Bountiful God,
you have blessed us in many ways,
in the beauty and richness of our land,
and in the freedom we enjoy.
You have given us even greater gifts
in our family who loves and cares for us
and in the grace which allows us to
know and believe in you.
May we be grateful for all our blessings,
not just today, but every day.
Help us to turn our gratitude into action
by caring for those in need
and by working for a more just society.
Bless this wonderful meal before us and each of us at this table.
Be with all those we love who are not here.
We give you thanks through Jesus our Lord.
Amen.

LET'S SAY GRACE

# November 29
## Dorothy Day

Dorothy Day, who died on this date in 1980, dedicated her life to serving Christ by serving the poor. After a bohemian youth she converted to Catholicism and, with Peter Maurin, began the Catholic Worker movement. A newspaper, *The Catholic Worker*, was also established to promote the peace and rights of workers. The newspaper remains in existence today and Catholic Worker Hospitality Houses continue to shelter the homeless and feed the hungry.

God of the poor,
you gave Dorothy Day the grace
to recognize the face of Jesus
in the penniless, the hungry, and the homeless.
May your Spirit guide us to recognize Jesus
in the people we meet each day.
Whether they hunger for food
or for friendship,
help us to find ways
to respond to their needs.
Bless this food we share.
Help us to thank you at all times,
whether in want or in plenty,
through Christ our Lord.
Amen.

*Holy Days and Holidays*

# December 2
## The Martyrs of El Salvador

On December 2, 1980, Maryknoll sisters Maura Clarke and Ita Ford, Ursuline sister Dorothy Kazel, and lay missioner Jean Donovan—all Americans—were brutally murdered in El Salvador. Like many other Latin American martyrs before and since, their only crime was to serve the poor and preach the gospel.

God of justice,
your love overcomes the power of evil
through forgiveness and compassion.
As we remember the courage
of Maura, Ita, Dorothy, and Jean,
inspire us to be witnesses
to the coming of your kingdom
through our service to those in need
and our commitment to live the truth of the gospel.
As we share this meal,
bless us with the awareness of all those who are hungry,
and all those who struggle for justice and truth.
We ask this in the name of Jesus,
whose coming we await with hope.
Amen.

# December 6
## Nicholas

A fourth-century bishop from Asia Minor, St. Nicholas is the patron of children and the inspiration behind Santa Claus. Known for his acts of charity, Nicholas often secretly left gifts of food or money for the poor in the dark of night, so that no one but God could see his good works. In many countries on December 6 children put shoes outside their doors to be filled with treats.

Gentle God,
you gave St. Nicholas
a generous heart
to care for those in need.
As we prepare for Christmas,
we remember his kindness
and imitate his generosity
as we select gifts for
our friends and family.
Help us to be generous,
not only to our loved ones,
but to all who are in need.
Bless this meal.
May our sharing make us ready
to welcome Jesus
when he comes to us this Christmas.
Amen.

*Holy Days and Holidays*

# December 8
# The Immaculate Conception

This feast is not the commemoration of Jesus' conception, but of Mary's. Although Joachim and Ann are not named in the Bible, an ancient tradition holds that they were Mary's parents. The church holds that Mary was conceived by her parents in the natural human way, but that she was conceived without original sin. This is a gift that God gave her in anticipation of her Son's redemption. God's grace enabled Mary to live her entire life without ever sinning. Mary is revered as the patroness of the United States under this title.

O God,
your love is always with us,
from the first moment of our lives until the last.
As you kept Mary always close to you,
never let us stray from the way you have prepared for us.
Make our hearts open like hers
to receive the gift of Jesus' love.
May this meal that we share
prepare us to greet him when he comes.
Bless our food, our conversation,
and the love we share in Jesus' name.
Amen.

# December 10
## Thomas Merton

As a young man, Thomas Merton experienced a profound conversion that led him to become a Trappist monk. His life and many books about the spiritual life have inspired millions of people. Just before his death on December 10, 1968 he spoke these words: "What we are asked to do is not so much to speak of Christ, but to let him live in us."

God of light and darkness,
your love is present always,
calling us to yourself in everything we do.
We thank you for the many gifts
you gave Thomas Merton
to make him a guide for us as
we seek your presence.
During this season of Advent
give us the grace to wait patiently
for your coming,
and make us alert to your
Spirit's every move.
May our hunger for this meal
remind us of our hunger for you.
Bless this food and all who seek your face.
Amen.

# December 12
## Our Lady of Guadalupe

In 1531 Mary appeared to an Indian named Juan Diego in Tepeyac, Mexico. When asked by the bishop to produce proof of her appearance, he took off his cloak and found that the image of the Virgin was emblazoned on it. This cloak with its image can still be seen today in the church built upon the place of the apparition. Our Lady of Guadalupe is the patroness of the Americas.

Loving God
you choose the poor and simple ones of the world
to proclaim the good news of your presence among us.
Just as Jesus was first revealed to the shepherds,
so too Mary made herself known through Juan Diego.
Make us poor in spirit and pure of heart
so that we may be ready to welcome you when you come.
We thank you for this food before us,
and for all the gifts we receive from your goodness
through Christ our Lord.
Amen.

# December 13
## Lucy

St. Lucy lived on the island of Sicily. Around the year 304 she was put to death because of her faith by the Roman emperor Diocletian. Her name means "light," and because this day was once the shortest of the year (before the calendar was revised) many celebrations grew up on December 13 to mark the beginning of longer days. In Scandinavia, where Lucy is greatly revered, young girls (representing Lucy) wear white dresses and wreaths on their heads with lit candles. They awaken their families to serve them coffee and a pastry called Lussekattor.

God of light,
during these days when the nights grow longer
we thank you for the gift of light
and for the warmth of your love.
Help us, like Lucy,
to be a sign of your light to others
and to share the joy we feel
as we prepare for the coming of Jesus.
Bless our meal and make us more aware
of those who are hungry or homeless
and of what we can do to help them.
We ask this through Christ our Lord.
Amen.

*Holy Days and Holidays*

# December 26
## Stephen

Because St. Stephen was the first Christian to die for the faith (his story is told in Acts 6 and 7), he is given the honor of being remembered on the day after Christmas. Stephen was one of the original seven deacons appointed by the apostles to take care of the needs of the poor in the church. Thus this day has been associated with serving the poor and the hungry, as the carol "Good King Wenceslaus" reminds us.

Faithful God,
you filled St. Stephen with the courage
to be a witness to Jesus despite his fears,
even his fear of death.
Give us the strength to be true signs of your presence,
even when, like Stephen,
we are rejected because of it.
As we share the gifts of this table
help us to remember those who have little during this season.
Teach us to reach out to them
with compassion and generosity.
We ask this in the name of Jesus,
our Savior and our friend.
Amen.

# December 27
## John

St. John is the second of the companions of Christ whose feast follows near to Christmas day. John's own gospel refers to him as "the disciple whom Jesus loved." The gospel of John is a very personal account of Jesus' life. It is sometimes called the "gospel of glory" because it sees in Jesus' earthly life the presence of the divine.

John's feast day is a good occasion to recall that of all the gifts we receive, the gift of Christian love is most precious.

God of love,
you gave St. John the gift of friendship with Jesus
and revealed to him that the love we share
is truly your presence among us.
We thank you for all the ways that your love comes to us,
especially through those who are gathered at this table.
We thank you for the food and drink we share,
and ask you to make us more mindful
of those who are hungry and thirsty.
We make this prayer through Jesus,
who is your love made visible in the world.
Amen.

# December 28
## The Holy Innocents

Matthew's gospel reports how in jealousy of the newborn Jesus, King Herod "ordered the massacre of all the boys in Bethlehem and its vicinity two years old and under" (2:16). Having been warned of this in a dream, Joseph took Mary and the baby and fled to Egypt. Jesus escaped, but those innocent little ones were the victims of Herod's insane fear.

Gracious God,
we pray for all those who suffer,
especially innocent children.
As you inspired Joseph to be the guardian of Jesus,
give us the wisdom and strength
to protect the life and well-being of children in need.
As we share this meal,
we thank you for your love
which sustains and strengthens us
to care for others and to work for justice.
We offer this prayer in Jesus' name.
Amen.

# TRADITIONAL
## GRACES

Bless us, O Lord, and these your gifts
which we are about to receive
from your bounty, through Christ our Lord. Amen.

God is great and God is good,
and we thank God for this food.
By God's hand must all be fed;
give us, Lord, our daily bread.
*The Hampton Grace*

Bless, O Lord, this food to our use,
and us to your loving service.
Make us ever mindful to the needs of others
in the name of Jesus Christ. Amen.

Blessed are you, Lord our God,
Creator of the universe!
Through your word all things were made
and by your goodness we have this food to share.
Blessed be God forever.
*Based on the Jewish blessing prayer, the Berakah*

The eyes of all wait upon you, O Lord,
and you give them their food in due season.
You open your hand
and fill every living thing with your blessing.

We thank you, O Lord, for these
your gifts
and ask you to grant
that whether we eat or drink, or whatever we do,
we do it for your glory.

*The Roman Ritual, based on Psalm 104:27-28*
*and 1 Corinthians 10:31*

Give food to the hungry, O Lord,
and hunger for you to those who have food.

Now that I am about to eat, O great Spirit,
I give my thanks to the beasts and birds
whom you have provided for my hunger,
and pray deliver my sorrow that living things
must make a sacrifice for my comfort and well-being.

LET'S SAY GRACE

Let the feather of corn spring up in its time,
and let it not wither, but make full grains
for the fires of our cooking pots,
now that I am about to eat.

*A Native American grace from the Lama*
*Foundation, San Cristobal, New Mexico*

Be present at our table, Lord.
Be here and everywhere adored.
Thy creatures bless, and grant that we
may feast in paradise with Thee.

*John Wesley*

May the blessing of God rest upon you,
May God's peace abide with you.
May God's presence illuminate your heart
now and forever more.

*A Sufi Blessing*

We being many are one bread, and one body;
for we are all partakers of that one bread.
Whether therefore you eat, or drink,
or whatever you do, do all to the glory of God.
*Based on 1 Corinthians 10:17, 31*

Give us grateful hearts, our Father,
for all your mercies,
and make us mindful of the needs of others.
*Book of Common Prayer*

For each new morning with its light . . .
for rest and shelter of the night,
for health and food, for love and friends,
for everything Thy goodness sends.
*Ralph Waldo Emerson*

Now thank we all our God,
with heart and hand and voices
who wondrous things hath done,
in whom his world rejoices.
*Catherine Winkworth*

LET'S SAY GRACE

Thank you, God, for food so good,
Lord help us do the things we should.

God in me and God in you
there lies all the good we do.
We thank you, Lord, that this is so,
we thank you that we live and grow.

Bendecimos, Señor, a nosotros.
Bendice estos alimentos que vamos a tomar.
Bendice a quienes los han preparado.
Dales pan a los que tienen hambre,
y hambre y sed de justicia a los que tenemos pan.
Te lo pedimos por Cristo nuestro Señor. Amen.
*Traditional Spanish grace*

Bendigamos al Señor, que nos une en caridad
y nos nutre con su amor, en el pan de la unidad,
O Padre nuestro.
*Traditional Spanish hymn*

**Robert M. Hamma** is the author of *Come to Me* a collection of prayers during time of illness, and *Together at Baptism*, a catechesis for parents who are preparing their children for baptism. He and his wife Kathryn have three children—Peter, Christine, and Sarah—and have co-authored several articles about celebrating the feasts and seasons of the liturgical year at home.